SENTIMENT OF FLOWERS

Material: Rocket larkspur, carnation, great cattail, Japanese yellow cypress, clematis, ibota privet, evergreen spindle tree
Container: Brown glazed compote

花の思い

花材　千鳥草、カーネーション、がま、まさき、黄金ひば、いぼた、てっせん
花器　茶釉黒紋コンポート

やさしい千鳥草の表情にはわずかながられいが感じられ、明るくすなおな少女のようなカーネーションはほほえむように愛らしい。

千鳥草には内気な花の思いがあり、カーネーションにはあどけない花の恋心がある。そしてクっセんには、ときにとらわれる寂しい物思いがある。

心に秘めごとを持ち始めた年ごろの少女を思わせる三つの花たち。

明るいはなやぎのなかにも感傷的なけはいがただよう。

立て方
① すなおに伸びた千鳥草を垂直に立てる。
② ①と同じ長さの千鳥草を右のほうへ傾ける。
③ ①の左うしろ角に長短のバランスを考えて3本のカーネーションとがまの葉をさす。
④ 左にまさきをさし出す。
⑤ 黄金ひばで中央下段の量感を出す。
⑥ 右前角にいぼたをさす。
⑦ つき葉を生かしたクっセんで、水ぎわを引きしめる。

The gentle rocket larkspur is slightly melancholic while the carnations are quite sweet, like bright and pliable young girls.

There is the shy sentiment of a flower in the rocket larkspur and in the carnation there is an unsophisticated awakening of love. Clematis is in a pensive mood, lonely perhaps anticipating its evanescence.

These three different flowers bring forth the image of girls in their adolescence, beginning to have a secret in their hearts.

Melancholic sentiment lingers somewhere in the atmosphere, though it be gay and brilliant.

Method:
1. Stand straight a stalk of slender and facilely tall rocket larkspur.
2. Slant another stalk of rocket larkspur of the same length as (1) to the right.
3. Provide three stalks of carnations and a great cattail leaf at the rear corner to the left of (1), giving care to the proportioning of the lengths.
4. Arrange a branch of evergreen spindle tree on the left.
5. The effect of massiveness is created by the placement of the Japanese yellow cypress at the base in the center.
6. Place the ibota privet on the right-front corner.
7. The clematis with its leaves gives a bracing effect to the waterside.

MUTUAL RESPONSE

Material: Calla lily, zebra grass, anthrium, golden banded lily, gentian
Container: Brown glazed compote

呼応する姿

花材　カラー、矢はずすすき、アンスリウム、
　　　山ゆり、玉りんどう
花器　茶釉押紋コンポート

細い葉先が風の中にすうっと消えてしまいそうなすすきと、みずみずしい美しさを見せるカラーの出合いには、しずかな中に、やさしいったわりの感情が通うように思われる。

カラーとすすきと添うず離れず寄り添うアンスリウム、下から首を上げて呼びかけるアンスリウム、鮮烈な花色とかたい茎が強い意志を感じさせるものの、何かを求めているようだ。

花には花の思いがあって、互いに呼応しながら生きているのかもしれない。すすき、カラー、アンスリウムが求め合うように揺れ動く姿に、大きなゆりの花とわずかに見せた王りんどうの紫で均衡を保った。

立て方
① カラーは、茎の自然なカーブを生かして立てる。
② 矢はすすきの葉は、1枚は側面を見せて左うしろ角へ思い切り長く伸ばし、1枚は正面を見せて同じ方向へ振らす。残りの1枚は葉先をカットして、それぞれ異なった働きをあらわす。
③ アンスリウムは、花の面と茎の線を大胆に見せて左へ伸ばす。
④ 大輪の山ゆりを水ぎわ正面にさす。
⑤ 短くさし立てたカラーの花と、王りんどうをそえ、下段の力を補う。

Though quiet, the encounter of the zebra grass and the calla — the tips of the leaves of zebra grass looking as if they might vanish softly into the wind and the calla lily displaying its beauty so young and fresh — seems to embrace a tender communication of sympathy.

The calla lily and the zebra grass are snuggling against each other somewhat closely, but modestly, while the anthrium speaks to them from below, raising its head. The vivid coloring of the flower and the hard stem gives the impression of strong will, but at the same time seems to be searching for something.

It may perhaps be that flowers have their own sentiments and lead their own lives in sympathy with each other.

The rustling zebra grass, calla lily, anthrium, as if they are seeking each other, are balanced by the large lily and the purple of the gentian seen slightly to the rear.

Method:
1. Erect the calla, making the most of the natural curve of the stem.
2. One of the zebra grass leaves shows its edge stretching itself to the utmost towards the left rear corner. Another leaf dangles in the same direction, showing its surface. The tip of the remaining leaf is cut. Each leaf thus performes its own different function.
3. The anthrium stretches to the left boldly displaying the face of its flower and its stem line.
4. Arrange the large-flowered golden banded lily at the front edge of the water.
5. The short calla and gentian are arranged to further enhance the coloring and to supplement the strength of the lower part.

MORNING

Material: Great cattail, dahlia, damson, Chinese bell flower, false-spiraea, damson
Container: Blue glazed compote

朝

花材　がま、ダリア、すもも、ききょう、
　　　珍至梅
花器　青釉広口コンポート

まっすぐに伸びているのを、すぐな形のままに立てて、長短で変化をつけた花。夏の朝のこころよいしずけさを表現した。

1枚のがまを折ってみたが、折れたがまの葉が、すなおで軽やかなー瓶の中で、しずけさをいっそう感じさせるようだ。明るいダリアでも、ききょうととり合わせると、意外にしずかで、おもむきが感じられる。

立て方
①がまの葉2枚を立てる。1枚は伸びる力を見せ、1枚は上方で外側に折り曲げて屈折する形を見せる。
②垂直に立ったがまの葉に添わせて、長短2本のダリアをさす。
③ずもものの枝2本は、右側の空間に大きく働かせる。
④短いほうのダリアのうしろに、ききょう1輪を高くさし添える。
⑤珍至梅の花をマッスにして葉を添え、水ぎわをおだやかしくさしのえる。
⑥珍至梅の白い花色との対照を考えて、ききょう3輪を短くさす。

Those which have grown straight are erected in their straight form. Differences in lengths gives the variety. The pleasant serenity of a summer morning is presented in this arrangement.

A bent cattail leaf makes the atmosphere much more hushed and still about the gentle and cheerful vase. Even the bright dahlia is rendered unexpectedly quiet and composed when joined together with the Chinese bell flower.

Method:
1. Stand the two cattail leaves. One of them shows an extending movement and the other is bent to the outside at the upper section.
2. Two stalks of dahlias, one short and the other taller are arranged close to the straight standing cattail leaves.
3. Two damson branches function grandly in the space on the right.
4. The shorter dahlia is accompanied by a tall Chinese bell flower to the rear.
5. A mass of false-spiraea flowers accompanied with leaves is placed at the waterside to give a supporting touch.
6. Three Chinese bell flowers are put low to contrast with the white of the false-spiraea flowers

WIND OF VERDURE

Material: Striped bulrush, azalea, gladiolus, monstera, feather cockscomb
Container: Blue glazed compote

緑の風

花材　縞ふとい、つつじ、グラジオラス、モンステラ、やり鶏頭
花器　青釉コンポート

自然の働きには目を見張らせるものがある。魔術師の魔法のように次へ次へとこの大地にさまざまな美しい花や草木をつくり出してくれる。

描いたのかと思うほど鮮明な縞ぶとい白い横縞、鶏頭の赤、グラジオラスの黄、そしてモンステラの葉つき草木がこの地上にいっぱいあると思うだけでも心楽しい。

鶏頭とグラジオラスの赤と黄色が緑のなかでひときわ映えて、つつじの若葉に緑の風が感じられる。

立て方
①縞ぶとい数本を、前後左右に広がりを持たせてさすが、さし口は1本にまとめてまっすぐに立てる。
②①のうしろからつつじを高く立ててふといつつじを斜めに①の力を補う。低いつつじを前しろに振って奥行きを持たせ、同時に上段のつつじの力を受けさせる。
③①の前にやり鶏頭を立てる。
④黄色のグラジオラス2本を③の前に配して、やり鶏頭の力を補う。
⑤グラジオラスの花先の部分を見せて左下段に働かせる。
⑥モンステラの葉をカットして、面を見せ、前方へ振り出す。

There is something marvellous in the mechanisms of natural phenomena — creating each and every beautiful flower, grass and tree in great abundance on this mother earth.

The vividly white lateral stripes of the bulrush, the red colored feather cockscomb, the yellow of the gladiolus are as if someone has painted them, as do the cut-out lines of the leaves of the monstera. It gives one happiness to realize that the earth is rich with flowers, grasses and trees in infinite variety of color and pattern.

The red and yellow of the feather cockscomb and gladiolus cut a brilliant figure within the greenery. The young leaves of the azalea are suggestive of the wind passing through a green woods.

Method:
1. Stand several stalks of the striped bulrushes to curve outward in all directions. Put them together in a bundle at the base and let stand straight.
2. Arrange a branch of azalea up high behind (1) to enhance the strength of the bulrushes. A low dangling branch of azalea slanted at the rear contributes depth while at the same time supporting the authority of the azalea at the upper part.
3. Stand the cockscomb upright in front of (1).
4. Arrange two stalks of yellow gladiolus in front of (3) to supplement the force of the cockscomb.
5. Tip the gladiolus flower to the front so that it comes into play in the lower part.
6. Cut the monstera leaf and place it in order to make the surface show, thus making it appear to pop out.

YOUTHFULNESS

Material: Anthrium, zebra grass, croton, sunflower, hydrangea
Container: Boat-shaped vase

若い人

花材　アンスリウム、矢はずすすき、クロトン、ひまわり、あじさい
花器　焼きしめ船形鉢

つゆが明けると、街は急に活気づいてくる。赤や青や黄などとりどりの洋服をつけた若い人たちの個性的な姿が急に目立つようになる。大胆な服を着こなして、さわやかに街を行く彼らの姿は、美しい。

色も形もはっきりとしていて個性が強いアンスリウム、ひまわり、あじさいをとり合わせて、「若い人」と題した。

アンスリウムとクロトンの間になびく矢はすすきも若々しく感じられ、現代的な香りでいっぱいの明るい花になった。

立て方
① アンスリウムは、技巧をこらさずに立てる。
② すすきは3枚の葉を残して他は整理し、茎の力強さを見せて①の右に立てる。
③ ①の前に低くひまわりをさす。
④ 2本のあじさいを手前下段にさし、上段の動きをととのえる。
⑤ ②の横にクロトンの葉をさして、アンスリウムやひまわりとの力のバランスをはかり、全体の姿をととのえる。

When the rainy season is over, the streets are suddenly enlivened with young boys and girls in their attractive clothing mirroring their own originality in reds, blues, yellows. There is something refreshing about them and a beauty, too, when they wander the streets in the stylish clothes of bold design.

Under the banner of 'Youthfulness,' this combination was created with such flowers as anthrium, sunflower and hydrangea.

The zebra grass fluttering between anthrium and croton has an added freshness. The whole atmosphere is bright and filled with the smell of the modern.

Method:
1. Erect anthrium with no artifice.
2. Eliminate all but three leaves of zebra grass and stand them on the right of (1), emphasizing the strength of the stem.
3. Place the sunflower low in front of (1).
4. Put two stalks of hydrangea at the bottom front as accessory.
5. Insert the croton beside (2) to balance the forces created by anthrium and sunflower. Correct the overall appearance.

VIGOR

Material: Giant reed, bulrush, Hanson's lily, croton, evergreen spindle tree, calla lily, rose
Container: Brown glazed compote

勢い

花材 だんちく、ふとい、竹島ゆり、クロトン、カラー、まさき、ばら
花器 茶釉コンポート

同じ花や草木でも、その姿勢によって感じ方が異なる。

1本のだんちくで4枚の葉を生かしたが、一方はなびかせ、一方は葉先をカットしてみた。なびく姿には、目に見えない風が感じられ、やさしい趣があらわれた。カットしたほうの葉にはだんちくの強い生命力と鋭い気迫があらわれた。

3本のふとい、その間隔に差をつけて傾斜させると、走り出すような勢いが感じられる。水辺でしずかに立ちすくんでいるふとい。その上からは想像できない積極性である。上段のだんちくとふとい、クロトンにもある力にささえられて、空間に存分に動きを見せている。可憐な花をあしらって、いろどりとやさしさを添えてみた。

立て方
① だんちくは、葉に表情を持たせて、上段の空間を構成する。
② 竹島ゆりの1本を高くさす。
③ 花の姿を色を生かして、もう1本を低くさす。
④ ふとい3本を左へ鋭く振り出す。
⑤ クロトン2枚は葉を向かい合わせ、だんちくと竹島ゆりを囲むようにさす。
⑥ カラーの花2本を前方へさす。
⑦ ばらとまさきを⑥の左右うしろ脇にさし、下段をととのえて仕上げる。

The impression is different even if the same flowers and grasses are used, if they have different shapes.

Four leaves from a stalk of the giant reed were used: make two on one side look as if they were bending to the wind and cut off the ends of the other two on the opposite side. The bending leaves show us the invisible wind while the cut leaves indicate the strong vitality and intrepid spirit of the giant reed.

Even the three bulrushes, which look powerful enough, suddenly start running, when slanted at different intervals. There is a positiveness, something which cannot be imagined, in the bulrushes standing quiet straight at the waterside. The giant reed and bulrushes at the upper part are swaying freely in the air, supported by the potential energy of the crotons. The pretty flowers are located so as to add colorfulness and tenderness.

Method:
1. The giant reed defines the upper space with the expressiveness of its leaves.
2. One stalk of Hanson's lily is stood high.
3. Another flower stalk of Hanson's lily stands low.
4. Three stalks of bulrushes are swung sharply to the left.
5. Arrange two croton leaves face to face as if enclosing the giant reed and Hanson's lily.
6. Arrange two stalks of calla luly in front.
7. Put a rose and a branch of evergreen spindle in the left and right rear of (6).

GROWING TALLER

Material: Chinese bell flower, allium, fringed iris, spiraea thunbergii, dahlia, vaccinium oldhami, thunberg lily
Container: Deep brown glazed pot

伸びる姿

花材　ききょう、アリウム、しゃが、雪柳、
　　　ダリア、夏はぜ、すかしゆり
花器　茶釉深鉢

花や草木が伸びる姿はさまざまである。すなおに行儀よく伸びるきもあろう、たくましく一息に伸びて、なお力の余裕あるアリウム、はずみがあり、リズムを感じさせる雪柳のきゃしゃな枝――伸びる姿のなかにそれぞれのふぜいを感じさせてくれる。

たくましく、あるいはやさしく、はずみつつ伸びる花や草木の動きを一瓶の中で調和させ、それぞれのふぜいを生かして構成するのはたのしいものだ。しかしわずかな部分からその動きと趣きをとらえるためには、その花材のよさを生かそうとする心がなくてはできないのではないだろうか。

立て方
① すなおに伸びたきょうを高く立てる。
② 曲がりのおもしろいアリウムを、きをうに添わせる。
③ 雪柳は、わずかに間をおいて①と②に添う姿でゆったり立てる。
④ 左後方へ向け、しゃがの葉数枚をなびかせる。
⑤ ①の前へきょうを低く立てる。
⑥ 夏はぜは枝ぶりのおもしろさを生かし、枝先をうしろへ振って奥行きをはかる。
⑦ ⑤の前へダリアをさす。
⑧ すかしゆりの花で全体を引きしめる。

Flowers, grasses and trees grow in different ways. The Chinese bell flowers, obedient and mannerly, stand high. The strong allium grows straight out, the vigor being so abundant that much energy is left even after its rapid growth. The delicate branches of spiraea thunbergii are springy and rhythmical. Thus each has its own individual charm in the way it grows.

It is indeed a joy to make a composition by harmonizing the different movements of these flowers, grasses and trees some growing vigorously, others gently and still others flexibly. If we are prepared to make the most of each material, only a small part is enough to grasp the unique movement and charm of the material.

Method:
1. Place upright a tall stalk of pliable Chinese bell flowers.
2. Place the allium in an interesting form bending close to the Chinese bell flower.
3. Place also a branch of the spiraea thunbergii to snuggle against (1) and (2), leaving a little space around them.
4. Let several leaves of fringed iris to flutter toward the rear left.
5. Stand a stalk of Chinese bell flower low in front of (1).
6. By vivifying the exquisiteness of the shape of the vaccinium oldhami, fling the top of the branch to the rear to build depth.
7. Place the dahlia in front of (5).
8. Give a finishing touch to the whole with a thunberg lily.

A MOMENT OF TRANQUILITY

Material: Lotus, plantain lily, zebra grass, thunberg lily, liatris
Container: Scarlet glazed bottle

静寂のとき

花材　はす、ぎぼうし、矢はずすすき、すかしゆり、リアトリス
花器　朱釉金紋瓶

真夏の昼さがり、風も音も、消えてしまった静寂の一瞬を、はすを主材としていけてみた。

はす一色の立華は伝統花とされる。花や葉の生育状態をよく観察し、それぞれの姿かたちの美しさを十分生かして使いわけ、一瓶の花としてのえるものである。

はすの開花は低く、つぼみは高くきすのが、はす一色の使い方であるが、ここではゆりの開花を使ってみた。ひとつしのの葉のかすかな枯れ色も、どりどりとして働いている。

立て方
① はすのつぼみを垂直に立てる。
② ①に添わせて矢はすすきを立てる。葉の1枚は前方になびかせ、3枚は左のやや前後になびかせて、上段におおらかな空間を構成する。
③ 2枚のきぼうしの葉面を、中段から下段に見せて、奥行きを持たせる。2枚が同じ表情にならないように。
④ はすのつぼみと巻き葉を①の前に短く立て。
⑤ はすの葉1枚は、茎にはずみをつけ（18番程度のもの）を入れてはずみの葉より前の角きに、矢はずすきの葉より上向度に振り出す。
⑥ 黄色のすかしゆりを1輪、花の正面に見せてさし、全体を引きしめる。
⑦ 矢はずすきをはすの葉の空間に、リアトリスをあしらって姿をととのえる。

An instant of quiet with no wind and no sound is expressed through the lotus, as the primary material.

A *rikka* of monochrome lotus is required by tradition. The arrangement is created by closely observing the conditions of the growth of the flowers and leaves, and then correctly utilizing each shape and form to the full.

The customary method of arranging the lotus is to place the bud high and the flower low. However, here a thunberg lily in bloom is used. The withering leaves of plantain lily is another addition of coloring.

Method:
1. Stand the lotus bud upright.
2. Place the zebra grasses to snuggle against (1). One of the leaves bends to the front and the other three to the left so as to provide ample space in the upper part.
3. The effect of massiveness as well as depth is created from the middle to the bottom parts by using two plantain lily leaves. Care is to be taken that the two leaves do not have the same expression.
4. Stand the bud low and the rolled leaf of the lotus in front of (1).
5. One of the lotus leaves is given bounce with a piece of wire (about No.18 in gauge) inserted inside the stem so that it springs out at an angle facing upward in front of the zebra grass.
6. Insert one stalk of yellow thunberg lily to face the front, thus giving a finishing touch to the arrangement.
7. The gap between zebra grass and lotus leaves is filled with liatris, thus balancing the overall composition.

SUMMER FESTIVAL

Material: Variegated lily, giant reed, liatris, European mountain ash, vaccinium oldhami, Japanese cypress, dahlia, small chrysanthemum, Solomon's seal, spiraea thunbergii
Container: White glazed pot with purple flambé

夏祭り

花材　かのこゆり、だんちく、リアトリス、ななかまど、夏はぜ、雪柳、ひば、ダリア、小菊、鳴子ゆり

花器　白釉紫ぼかし鉢

祭りは楽しい。ことに夏の祭りは、明るく開放的な気分が町や村いっぱいにあふれていて楽しいものだ。おとなも子どもも笑顔で言葉をかわす。その声にははずんだような響きが感じられる。

多種多様な花材を奔放な姿のままとり合わせ、一瓶にまとめて、「夏祭り」のイメージをあらわした。

花たちの笑い声が聞こえてくるようだ。

立て方
1. かのこゆりは、できるだけ高く立てる。
2. ①の高さと傾きに合わせて、だんちく を立てる。
3. ななかまどは、右うしろ角へ向ける。
4. リアトリス2本を中央に垂直に立てる。
5. 夏はぜの枝2本を左うしろ角に向け、興行きを持たせる。
6. 左うしろ角へ雪柳を振って、③とのバランスをはかる。
7. ひばを③の下にあしらう。
8. 大輪のダリアを低くさす。前方やや左へ傾けて、強い印象を弱める。
9. 小菊はマッスにして手前から⑦の下へかけてゆるやかにあしらう。
10. 鳴子ゆりをあしらって、下段をととのえ、仕上げる。

Merry are the festivals. The summer festivals are especially so, since the villages and towns are filled with pleasant open-hearted greetings. The grown-ups and the children all exchange greetings, with beaming smiles and animated voices.

The image of 'summer festival' is brought about with an assortment of diverse flowers and grasses as materials in their natural and willful forms in one container.

Listen! Joyous laughing voices are heard. Or is it merely our fancy?

Method:
1. Erect a showy lily as high as possible.
2. Stand a stalk of giant reed to conform with the angle of (1).
3. A branch of European mountain ash is faced to the rear right corner.
4. Set two stalks of liatris vertical at the center.
5. Two branches of vaccinium oldhami are to face the rear left corner to add depth.
6. A branch of spiraea thunbergii is dangled to the left rear to balance (3).
7. Arrange the Japanese cypress at the bottom of (3).
8. Put a large flowered dahlia to jut out low, slightly slanted to the left in front.
9. Arrange a mass of small chrysanthemums in front and below (7).
10. Lastly, a finishing touch is given by a Solomon's seal, placed at the base.

IMPRESSIONS OF A SUNFLOWER

Material: Great cattail, liatris, vaccinium oldhami, spleenwort, sunflower, plantain lily and gentian
Container: Iron grained compote

ひまわりの印象

花材　がま、リアトリス、夏はぜ、谷渡り、
　　　ひまわり、ぎぼうし、りんどう
花器　鉄釉コンポート

がまも夏はぜも、花材としてはおとなしく地味な味わいのものである。夏の花であるリアトリスも比較的おとなしい。そうした地味なとり合わせの中に、太陽そのもののようなひまわりの鮮明な花色と明確な形を少しのぞかせた。

ゆったりと立ち伸びるがまも夏はぜもその動きの中に一瞬静止した姿が見られる。動きを始めるときに見せるごくわずかな静止の瞬間と、動きやんだその瞬間には、内に大きな力がこもっている。しずかなたたずまいのうちにある草木の力とひまわりの強烈な印象とをあらわしてみた。

花をいけるとき、とり合わせる花材は作意によってきまるのだが、ときには花材を見て、いけようという気持ちが誘わわれることもあり、またあるときは花器によって誘われることもある。

立て方

① ゆったりと伸びるがまを立てる。
② 夏はぜは左へ振り出して枝を整理する。
③ リアトリス 3 本をがまの前に立てる。
④ 谷渡りを右うしろ角へ向けて 1 枚振り出す。
⑤ ひまわりをとりどり各 1 本を低く前方に配す。
⑥ ぎぼうしの葉は正面を見せてひまわりにかかるようにさし、全体を引きしめる。

Both great cattail and vaccinium oldhami are quiet and modest in character. Liatris, a summer flower, is also a gentle type. From inside the combination of all these simple materials, the bright color and vivid form of a sunflower, a replica of the sun itself, peeps out.

When arranging flowers, materials are usually selected from a creative impulse. However, at times the concept to create a work is aroused by seeing certain materials and at other times by a container.

Method:
1. Erect the facilely stretching great cattail leaves.
2. Place a branch of vaccinium oldhami to swing to the left, and trim.
3. Erect three stalks of liatris in front of the great cattails.
4. Arrange one spleenwort toward the rear corner on the right.
5. Arrange one stalk each of sunflower and gentian at the front part to come out low.
6. Insert a leaf of plantain lily with the front shown and cover the sunflower partly.

HARMONY

Material: Great cattail, bulrush, thunberg lily, croton, plum, pink, vaccinium old-hami
Container: Brown glazed compote

調　和

花材　がま、五月梅、ふとい、すかしゆり、
　　　クロトン、なでしこ、夏はぜ
花器　茶釉縦縞紋コンポート

いけばなでは花材の個性を生かすことがたいせつだが、ことに立華はあれこれと花材のとり合わせをすることの楽しみが大きい。花材がそれぞれの個性を十分発揮し、総合されて美しいものに仕上がったときの喜びは言葉には尽くせない。ゆったりとおおらかに伸びるがま、細い枝ながらはずみのある五月梅、シャープな線が美しいふとい、この三つの花材で大きく空間を構成し、中央を力強いクロトンで引きしめた。水ぎわは軽やかになでしこを添えてみると、ゆったりとした姿のなかに何か心楽しいリズムが感じられるものになった。

いける楽しさをそのまま作品にあらわせたときは、見る人にもその楽しさが伝わるように思う。

立て方
① がまの葉数枚は、垂直に立てる。1枚の葉先に大きな動きを見せる。
② 五月梅の枝は、はずみを生かして葉の整理をし、右へ向かわせる。
③ ふとい は、水ぎわから左うしろ角へ勢いを感じさせるように走らせる。
④ あをやかなかしゆりをがまの前にさす。
⑤ クロトンを中段から下段に配して量感を出す。
⑥ なでしこをあしらっていろどり、姿をととのえる。
⑦ 夏はせずで水ぎわを軽快にまとめて仕上げる。

It is important in the flower arrangement to make the most of the peculiarity of each material. In *rikka*, there is special enjoyment in selecting an assortment of materials and trying various combinations.

The placidly stretching great cattails, plum looking springy though twiggy, and bulrush with its beautifully sharp lines, these three materials were used to delineate a huge space with the powerful croton giving firmness in the center. The waterside is lightly accentuated with vaccinium oldhami. When pinks are added for coloring the whole atmosphere takes on a placid look, and even a cheerful rhythm is expressed in the work itself, that joy may perhaps be communicated to the viewers.

Method:
1. Stand several great cattail leaves vertically. One of the leaves is made to take on great movement.
2. By utilizing the springiness of the branch, the plum is turned to the right with any unnecessary leaves removed.
3. Bulrushes are placed from the edge of the water to the rear corner on the left in a dashing manner to express vigor.
4. Insert a small stalk of thunberg lily in front of the great cattails.
5. Croton is arranged between the middle and the lower parts to produce massiveness.
6. Pinks are used to add color and to correct the overall form.
7. The water surface is finished neatly with vaccinium oldhami.

SHOWING SIGNS OF FLYING AWAY

Material: Flax lily, fringed iris, anthrium, gladiolus, calla lily
Container: Blue grey glazed compote

飛び立つけはい

花材　ニューサイラン、しゃが、アンスリウム、グラジオラス、カラー
花器　灰青釉コンポート

ニューサイランのすっきりとした直線には、切れるような鋭どさが感じられる。アンスリウムには、かたく強い持有の表情がある。ニューサイランにアンスリウムを添わせて立ち伸びる姿に構成すると、二つの個性があいまって、空に向かって何かが飛び立つようすかけはいうか出てきた。

水ぎわのカラーと下段のグラジオラスで、飛び立つものが、一瞬身をかがめて力を込める姿勢をあらわしてみた。省略された形の中にこもる勢いと力をあらわしてみた。しかしそれでもやはり、やさしい明るいものが全体を包んでしまうのは植物特有の味わいであろう。

一瓶のいけばなによるのではなく、生命ある植物の息づかいによるものだと思う。

立て方

①ニューサイランは面を見せて、長い1枚は葉先を右へくらせ、短いほうは鋭く、ややたへ傾けて立てる。
②アンスリウム1本を左へさし立てる。
③しゃがの葉を右うしろ角になびかせて奥行きをはかり、中段の空間を構成する。
④ニューサイランの前にグラジオラスを配し、いろどりと力を加える。
⑤カラーを正面に向けて低くさし、全体をひきしめる。

The slimly standing flax lily with its straight line has a cutting sharpness. The anthrium has a characteristic expression of solidness and mightiness. These two different individual characters combined — the anthrium close to the flax lily — create, hand in hand, a form of straight upright growth, a sign that something is going to fly away high into the sky.

The calla lily at the water surface and the gladiolus at the bottom show the posture of someone crouching just before putting forth all his strength and flying away. Concentrated vigor and strength are expressed and abbreviated in a simple form. However, there is still a tender and bright feeling embracing the whole atmosphere thanks to the fact that the setting is all vegetation. The comforts are given by the flowers in a vase not because of their appearance but because of the breath of the living vegetation.

Method:
1. A long leaf of flax lily is placed upright showing the front surface while the shorter one is erected to slant a little to the left for a sharp edge.
2. Stand one flower stalk of anthrium on the left.
3. The middle space is defined by bending the fringed iris leaves from the right rear corner to create mass.
4. For additional color the gladiolus is arranged in front of the flax lily.
5. A calla lily inserted in the front gives a finishing touch to the water surface.

THE END OF SUMMER

Material: Bulrush, castor plant, liatris, vaccinium oldhami, chrysanthemum
Container: Blue glazed compote

夏の終わり

花材　ふとい、紅ひま、リアトリス、夏はぜ、
　　　菊
花器　青釉コンポート

水辺を思い、木陰の涼風を求めた夏も終わりに近づくと、秋が待ち遠しくなる。しかし、去りゆく季節が惜しまれる。秋には秋の姿に、夏は夏の草木のおい茂り、花や葉の草花が咲くく。花や草木のいろどりや姿が移り変わると、すれ違うように季節は移行し到来するを知る。私たちは季節の交替季節、そこには自然が繰り広げるドラマが感じられる。

太くたくましい茎にはっきりした形の葉をつけた紅ひま、細くきゃしゃくなし、すでに紅葉し始めた夏はぜ、そうした花材のもつ粗、密、強、弱の個性をとり合わせて、一瓶のなかに花をよせると、自然の景観が色濃くあらわれてくる。休にし、そのなかに花をひそとあらわれて、自然の景観が色濃くあらわれてくる。

立て方
① ふとい2本を長短にさし立てる。短いほうはうしろへ傾ける。
② 葉を整理して茎の線をすっきり見せた紅ひまを、①に添わせて左側に立てる。
③ もう1本の紅ひまは①のうしろをさし、短いふとい①の下で倒かをかせるが、大きい葉は整理しておく。
④ 紅葉した夏はぜ1枝を左の空間に働かせる。
⑤ 短めの夏はぜ1本を中央に低くかせる。
⑥ リアトリスを中央に低く立てる。
⑦ リアトリスの前方に菊をさす。
⑧ 夏はぜの小枝を⑦の前に張り出すようにさして下段の力とし、水ぎわを安定させる。全体にしたが強く、右側が比較的弱い感じになるから、右側にボリュームを持たせて調和をとる。

We fancied watersides and looked for shade under trees. But now the summer is almost over, we look forward to the coming of autumn, saying farewell to summer.

The castor plant with its big strong stem and leaves of clear-cut shapes, thin and slender bulrush, and vaccinium oldhami already in autumnal tints. This arrangement is an integrated combination of the roughness, fineness, strength and weakness, the varied individual characters of these materials. Natural scenery can be distinctly portrayed when grasses and trees are used as the main materials, with flowers placed quietly within.

Method:
1. Stand two stems of bulrush, one long and the other short, the latter slanting to the rear.
2. Erect a stalk of castor plant on the left side of (1) showing the prim line of the stem by eliminating superfluous leaves.
3. Another stalk of castor plant is put behind (1) to take its place below the short bulrush. Large leaves are to be removed.
4. One branch of the tinged vaccinium oldhami fills the space on the left side.
5. A shorter branch of vaccinium oldhami comes to the right.
6. Put a stalk of liatris in the center to protrude low.
7. Arrange the chrysanthemums in front of the liatris.
8. Arrange a small branch of vaccinium oldhami to stretch out in front of (7), giving force to the lower part, while stabilizing the waterside. Since the right looks comparatively weak while the left is strong, harmonize the overall form by giving more volume to the right.

ENSEMBLE OF LEAVES

Material: Great cattail, Japanese sago palm, dracena, strelitzia leaves, maple, patrinia, butcher's-broom
Container: Light brown compote

葉によるアンサンブル

花材　がま、そてつ、ドラセナ、ストレリチアの葉、かえで、なぎいかだ、おみなえし
花器　薄茶黒描紋コンポート

Leaves are extremely difficult to use.

A variety of leaves and grasses of different shapes are combined in this arrangement. Though there is no vivid color, each displays its own particular character. The longer one admires it the greater is the enjoyment, there being a good deal of charm in it.

Some may say that an arrangement of only leaves and grasses would lack any flavor. But addition of overly beautiful flowers should be avoided. The flowers of patrinia have unusual appearance, as the face of each flower is inconspicuous. Since the intention of this arrangement is to show the forms of leaves and grasses in full variety, the patrinia is an addition for a slight trace of coloring.

Method:
1. Stand a stalk of great cattail straight and arrange it so that the leaves seem to be moving in their upper parts.
2. Erect a stalk of Japanese sago palm beside the cattail leaves. Each slender leaf is to be clearly shown.
3. Use a discolored leaf of cattail to wave largely to the left.
4. Extend a strelitzia leaf to the rear corner on the right.
5. Insert a branch of maple under the cattail leaf to bend lightly towards the rear.
6. Stand dracena in front of (1). Care should be taken not to spread the leaves.
7. Arrange the butcher's-broom leaves to show their peculiarity at the base.
8. Add several stalks of patrinia between the butcher's-broom and dracena.

LIFE

Material: Bulrush, torch lily, oriental bittersweet, croton, hydrangea, sunflower
Container: White glazed compote

命

花材 ふとい、トリトマ、つるうめもどき、
　　　クロトン、あじさい、ひまわり
花器 白釉線紋薄端

16

すっかり日本の風土になじんだ花や草木でも、その姿をしのぶことができる。育てた風土をしのぶことができる。トリトマやクロトンもしさと南国の植物特有のたくましさがこもっている。ぶるしといけばな水辺を思わせるうもろこしは野山を思わせる。

それぞれが自分の育った環境をその姿いっぱいにあらわしている花や草木をより合わせて一瓶のいけばなに構成することは、たいへんむずかしいことだ。

ここでは、それぞれの植物が持に秘めている力と、伸びようとする勢いを美しいと思った。うちにあらわしてみたいと思った。鮮明な花色や、枝や葉の伸びやかな動きをまとめるのにさいので安定させ、品よくまとめてみた。個性の強いけ花材の果たす役割が大きい。

花器の形と色の取り合わせ

立て方
①ふとい2本を添わせながらやわらかくカーブをさせて立て、すなおな線の美しさをあらわす。
②花首の曲がったトリトマのおもしろい形を生かして、右うしろ角へ向けて垂直に立てる。
③まっすぐなトリトマの花を手前にさす。
④はずむ力感を見せてつるうめもどきを左へ働かせ、その勢いを上方に向ける。
⑤つるうめもどきの動きを合わせ、トリトマの力を受けるように、クロトンを配する。
⑥ふといとつるうめもどきの間にひまわり1本を低くくばらう。
⑦あじさいで水ぎわを引きしめ、全体の動きをささえる。

The torch lily and croton are of semi-tropical origins and have the strongness peculiar to plants of that clime. The bulrush calls to mind a waterside while the oriental bittersweet carries an image of hills and fields.

It would seem difficult to construct a composition of an assortment of flowers and plants which fully manifest their own original habitats.

Here, an experiment was made to express in striking color the powerful vitality and the vigor hidden in each plant. The vivid colors of the flowers and the facile motion of the branches and stems are stabilized with the hydrangea at the waterside, thus refining the whole arrangement.

The role of form and color of the container is paramount when the materials used are of marked individualities.

Method:
1. Let two stalks of bulrush snuggle against each other while showing a soft curve to express the beauty of their smooth lines.
2. Making the most of the interesting curve of the neck, stand a torch lily so as to face in the direction of the right-rear.
3. Place the straight torch lily lower in front.
4. Bring the springy branch of oriental bittersweet into play to the left. The force of the small branch is to look up toward the upper part.
5. Arrange a stalk of croton so that it absorbs the force of the torch lilies, while interacting with the motion of the bittersweet.
6. Place one sunflower to stick out low between the bulrush and the bittersweet.
7. Give a balancing touch to the water surface with the hydrangea to support the overall movement.

AUTUMN SKY

Material: Great cattail, giant reed, croton, liatris, stokesia, vaccinium oldhami, cattleya
Container: White glazed deep pot

秋の空

花材　がま、だんちく、クロトン、リアトリス、ストケシア、カトレア、夏はぜ
花器　白釉深鉢

秋には秋のしずかさはなやぎがある。高く澄みきった空に飛行機雲が白い線を描き、吹く風もさわやかな明るい秋の昼さがりの印象をあらわしてみた。

風にそよぐがまと、すっきりとしたた　へらくをとり合わせて、あでやかなカトレアにまとまりを求めた。ストケシアとリアトリスの色彩をあしらい、クロトンで全体を引きしめると、カトレアのイメージが変わり、しずかな花に見える。

このときクロトンの葉はそこになくてはならないもののように思える。

1輪の花、1枚の葉の存在がありがたく感じられるときこそ、その花材を生かしえたと言えるのではないだろうか。

立て方
①がまの葉1株のうち、1枚は垂直に立て、2枚は左方向へゆったりとのびさせる。
②だんちくの葉は①と対照的に扱って、勢いを感じさせる。
③クロトン2枚は、葉の表と裏を見せる。
④ストケシアをクロトンの左におしらう。
⑤リアトリスは、花色をきかせ、右うしろ角へ振る。
⑥カトレアを水ぎわにさし、花の正面を見せる。
⑦夏はぜの小枝を左脇に配して、下段のアクセントとする。

Though quiet, the autumn has its own gaiety. High above the clear blue sky white lines follow behind an airplane. Early afternoon of an autumn day when the cool breeze is breathing — an impression of bright autumn is expressed here.

With the leaves of the great cattail and the straight standing giant reeds combined the fascinating cattleya balances the whole. When the colors of the stokesia and liatris are added and the croton is used to brace the overall construction, the cattleya appears dignified and quiet.

It seems that in such arrangements the croton leaves are indispensable.

The materials can be brought to life only when every single flower and each leaf are esteemed to be precious. Is it not so?

Method:
1. Stand one leaf of the great cattail straight and extend the other two to the left, serenely and composedly.
2. The giant reeds are used in contrast with (1) to manifest vigor.
3. One of the croton leaves shows its face and the other its back.
4. Arrange the croton with the stokesia at the left side.
5. Emphasize the color of the liatris and extend it towards the rear right corner.
6. Insert a flower of cattleya at the water surface to face the front.
7. A twig of vaccinium oldhami is located on the left to give accent to the bottom.

SILENCE

Material: Eulalia, Japanese chestnut, dahlia, oriental bittersweet, gentian
Container: White glazed pot

しずまり

花材　すすき、栗、ダリア、つるうめもどき、りんどう
花器　白釉藍流し鉢

若者たちの色とりどりの服装や、明るい歌声でにぎわった夏山も、秋の訪れとともにしだいにおちつきをとりもどします。尾花が風に光り、りんどうの紫がさえるころ、秋の山には静寂のけはいが満ちてくる。紅葉のときを迎える前のひとときである。いっそうしっとりとすまり返った山肌に、つるもどきの朱が目にあざやかである。

小さな花器の上に、雄大な山の景観と情趣を再現し、そこに清澄な光を思うと、立華というものの魅力を思い知る。

立て方
①すすきの穂1本を垂直に立てる。
②左側の葉をカットしたすすきを①と同じ高さにさす。葉は奥行きや幅に変化をつけてなびかせる。
③栗を左へ振り出す。
④①②の前にすすきの穂の部分を低く垂直にさし加える。
⑤つるもどきは枝先をカットし、内にひそむ力を感じさせて右側の下段へ扱う。
⑥ダリアの花1輪を前方に向けて低くさし、全体をひきしめとのえる。
⑦りんどうは1本をすすきに添わせてまっすぐに、もう1本は③の下にさしおって、いろどりと下段の中心に力を添える。

When the heads of the Japanese pampas grass shimmer in the wind and the purple of the gentian is more vivid, the autumn mountain is dominated by tranquility. It is a brief space of time before the season of the autumn tints. The mountain surface is hushed and still where the scarlet of the oriental bittersweet is brilliant to the eyes.

Now the magnificent view and the charm of the mountains are reproduced in a small container. If you imagine the clear and lucid light glittering around those mountains and you will realize the magic charm of *rikka*.

Method:
1. Stand straight one stalk of the eulalia.
2. Erect another stalk of eulalia with the leaves cut off on its left side to stand the same height as (1). The leaves are extended backwards and sideways to give depth and breadth.
3. Extend a branch of the Japanese chestnut to the left.
4. Add a head of eulalia to stand straight in a low position.
5. Cut off the tip of a branch of the oriental bittersweet and arrange it before (1) and (2) at the lower right to show its hidden might.
6. Insert one flower of the dahlia low, facing front to balance the whole.
7. One stalk of gentian stands straight, close to the eulalia, and another comes under (3), to give the effect of coloring and at the same time strength in the center of the base.

A MOUNTAIN OF ROYAL PAULOWNIA

Material: Royal paulownia, fringed iris, maple, white camelia, young pine, small chrysanthemum, gentian
Container: White glazed pot

桐の山

花材 桐、しやが、かえで、つばき、若松、寒菊、りんどう
花器 白釉紫ぼかし鉢

桐の紅葉もすでに色あせた、寂しい晩秋。山の向こうではもう雪が降っているのだろうか。野山を飾っていた美しい花花もすっかり影をひそめて、これから植物にとっても寂しい季節が到来する。すっかり葉を落とした木々や霜にあらかたち下草の姿として、意志の強さがうかがわれる。どんな悪条件にもひるむことなく立ち向かって、その生命を全うしようとする意気込みをえ感じる。秋から冬にかけての草木のたたずまいを、桐としゃがを使って、豪快な動きのうちにあらわしてみた。

立て方

1. 二またに分かれた桐の1枝は、ややや左へ傾くように立てる。
2. 3枚の大きなしゃがの葉は、つやややかな面を見せて左方に大胆に扱う。
3. 大きな桐のつき枝を生かして、右へ豪快に張り出す。枝先は中心のほうへ向ける。
4. 白玉つばきは、葉を適当に整理して前方に立す。
5. 白玉つばきの花をぱん引き立せるように右に配す。
6. 葉菊2本は、若松で霜に枯れた姿を生かして、下段の左方にさす。
7. つばきの1枝に、虫食い葉のふぜいをあらわして右前方にさし出す。
8. (1)のうしろにもう1組のしゃがと、紅葉したかえでを配して興行きをはかる。
9. りんどうをあしらって、いろどりを添える。

It is already late autumn and lonesome, and the tinted leaves of the royal paulownias are discolored. Is it snowing beyond the mountain? The beautiful flowers decorating the fields and mountains have faded away and now it is the coming of a very strenuous season for plants.

The shapes of the naked trees and the grasses withered by frosts show the strength of their will. There is even an enthusiasm to stand against the severest of conditions with no wincing, to protect their very beings. The appearance of plants from autumn to winter is expressed in the grandeur of the movements of the royal paulownia and the fringed iris.

Method:
1. Erect a two-forked branch of the paulownia to slant slightly to the left.
2. Arrange the three large leaves of fringed iris boldly to the left showing their shiny surfaces.
3. By making the best use of *tsukieda* (an attached branch), stretch the large royal paulownia branch to the right in a stately manner. The branch tip is to face towards the center.
4. Erect a stalk of white camelia in front with the leaves properly trimmed.
5. To further enhance the elegance of the white camelia, arrange a branch of young pine behind it.
6. Put two stalks of small chrysanthemum at the bottom on the left, and emphasize their frost bitten appearance.
7. Stand a camelia branch with worm-eaten leaves in the right-front.
8. Arrange another set of fringed iris and the tinted maple behind (1) to create depth.
9. Use gentian to add another color.

A GARDEN IN WINTER

Material: Striped bamboo, royal paulownia, chrysanthemum, small chrysanthemum, pale broom, spiraea thunbergii
Container: White glazed indented pot

冬の庭

花材　くまざさ、雪柳、桐、石化えにしだ、
　　　菊、寒菊
花器　白釉ひねり鉢

色とりどりの花が咲いていた庭も、わずかに残り咲いている寒菊のほかには何もなくなってしまった。そんな冬の庭でひときわ美しく鮮明な姿に感じられるのがくまざさだ。くまざさは配材としてよく使われるが、ここでは主的に用いてみた。

立て方
① 3本のくまざさは、葉のおもしろさを生かして高く立てる。
② 雪柳は葉を整理して軽やかにさをを添わせ、上でゆるやかに離す。
③ くまざさのうしろと雪柳のうしろにえにしただを配して、力を補う。
④ 桐は力強く左へ振り出す。
⑤ ②の雪柳と呼応させて、低く雪柳をさす。
⑥ 葉の働きを考慮して、中輪の菊を2本さす。
⑦ 葉の茂った寒菊数本を⑥の前、横にさして水ぎわをととのえる。

Nothing but a few small chrysanthemums are left in the garden where the flowers of many colors were once blooming in all their brilliancy. The particularly and conspicuously beautiful figure in such a winter garden is the striped bamboo.

Though it is usually used as a supplement, here in this arrangement, it plays the major role.

Method:
1. Utilize the uniqueness of the leaves and erect three stalks of striped bamboo to stand high.
2. Remove the unnecessary leaves from a stalk of spiraea thunbergii and place it close to the right of (1), gradually separating toward the top to allow sufficient space between it and (1).
3. Arrange pale broom behind the striped bamboo and the spiraea thunbergii to give supplementary strength.
4. Extend a branch of royal paulownia to the left to show vigor.
5. Stand a short branch of spiraea thunbergii to act in concert with (2).
6. Two medium sized stalks of chrysanthemums are inserted, with due consideration to the movement of the leaves.
7. Give a finishing touch to the water surface by inserting several stalks of small chrysanthemums with a thick growth of leaves in front and on both sides of (6).